TESTIMONY OF LIFE

A SERVICE OF LESSONS AND CAROLS
CELEBRATING THE LIFE OF CHRIST

BY JOSEPH M. MARTIN
FULL ORCHESTRATION BY BRANT ADAMS
CHAMBER ORCHESTRATION BY KEITH CHRISTOPHER

① This symbol indicates a track number on the Studiotrax CD (Accompaniment Only), or SplitTrax CD.

SHAWNEE PRESS

EXCLUSIVELY DISTRIBUTED BY

HAL•LEONARD CORPORATION

7777 W. BLUEMOUND RD. P.O. BOX 13819 MILWAUKEE, WI 53213

Visit Shawnee Press Online at
www.shawneepress.com

FOREWORD

"Testimony of Life" is a worship cantata for Spring or anytime, inspired by the celebrated "lessons and carols" services most often associated with the Christmas season. This liturgical framework forms an excellent scaffold for the sharing of Scripture, prayers, narrations, choral anthems and congregational hymnody. I have adapted these elements of worship into a musical presentation that celebrates the life of Christ with an emphasis on His ministry, death and resurrection. Some may wish to present this work progressively throughout Lent, Holy Week and Eastertide. Others may perform it in its entirety as a concert piece or in a special worship gathering. In either case, it is my hope that this inclusive work will be an opportunity for all of your worshippers to be involved in the sharing of a meaningful acclamation of hope and grace.

Joseph M. Martin

(This may be read prior to the "Prologue," during the "Prologue" as printed in the score, or it may be printed in the program as a comtemplation preceding the beginning of the cantata.)

LESSON 1 (The Incarnation)

In the beginning was the Word, and the Word was with God, and the Word was God. He was with God in the beginning. Through Him all things were made; without Him nothing was made that has been made. In Him was life, and that life was the light of all the world. For God so loved the world that He gave His only begotten Son, that whosoever believeth in Him should not perish but have everlasting life.
John 1:1-4; 3:16

PROLOGUE

Words by
FANNY J. CROSBY (1820-1915)

Music by
JOSEPH M. MARTIN (BMI)
Incorporating tunes:
STORY OF JESUS
and **LOVE OF GOD**

* Tune: STORY OF JESUS, John R. Sweney, 1837-1899
Words: Fanny J. Crosby, 1820-1915

sweet - est that ev - er was heard.   Sweet - est that ev - er was

heard

NARRATOR:
In the beginning was the Word, and the Word was with God...

② Not too fast, with sensitivity (♩ = ca. 74)

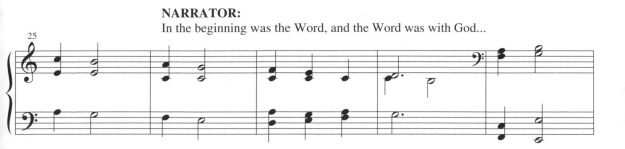

* Tune: LOVE OF GOD, Frederick M. Lehman, 1868-1953   TESTIMONY OF LIFE - SATB

and the Word was God.

33 He was with God in the beginning.

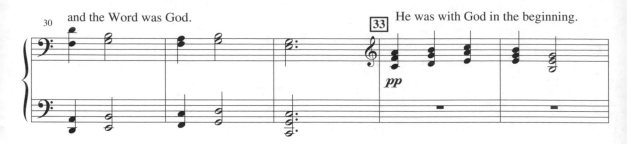

Through Him all things were made; without Him nothing was made that has been made. In Him was

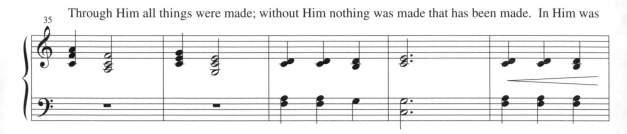

life, and that life was the light of all the world. For God so loved the world that He gave His

only begotten Son, that whosoever believeth in Him should not perish but have everlasting life.

48 **Boldly moving ahead (♩ = ca. 82)**

67 Slower, like a distant memory

I WILL SING THE WONDROUS STORY

(Congregational Anthem and Processional) *

Words by
FRANCIS H. ROWLEY (1854-1952)

Tune: **HYFRYDOL**
by ROWLAND H. PRICHARD (1811-1887)
Arranged by
JOSEPH M. MARTIN (BMI)

* Part for congregation is on page 84.

9

TESTIMONY OF LIFE - SATB

found___ me; found the sheep___ that went___ a-
o'er___ me. Sor - row's paths___ I of - ten

stray,_____ threw___ His lov - ing arms___ a-
tread;_____ but___ the Sav - ior still___ is

round___ me, drew___ me back___ in - to His way.
with___ me. By___ His hand___ I'm safe - ly led.

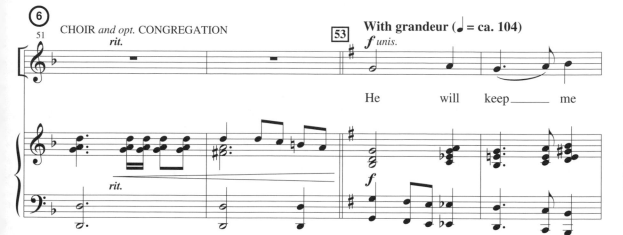

CHOIR *and opt.* CONGREGATION

With grandeur (♩ = ca. 104)

He will keep me

till the riv - er rolls its wa - ters at my

feet. Then He'll bear me safe - ly o - ver,

Sing with the saints in glo - ry, gath - ered

Sing it with the saints in glo - ry, gath - ered

by the crys - tal sea.

end descant

by the crys - tal sea.

end congregation

CHOIR *only*

S. *rit.*

A.

I will sing! I will sing!

T.

rit.

B.

PRAYER *(optional)*

God is seeking us. God is speaking to us. God is reaching out to us through the life of His Son, Jesus. We gather today to share the music of promise and to renew our hope in God's unfailing love. We join our hearts in worship, to celebrate the grace that transforms us and to offer testimony to the life that forever changed the world. O God, Creator of all that is joy and all that is truth, we present our hearts in thanksgiving for the gift of alleluia. We offer our prayers of gratitude and devotion in the words taught to us by Jesus praying... Our Father, who art in heaven... (The Lord's Prayer)

LESSON 2 (The Young Jesus in the Temple)

When Jesus was twelve years old, His parents went to Jerusalem for the Festival of the Passover according to the custom. When Passover was over, Jesus' relatives and friends set out to return home. However, they were not aware that the boy Jesus had stayed behind in Jerusalem. When His parents could not find Him, they went back to Jerusalem to search for Him.

After three days, they found Him in the temple courts, sitting among the teachers, listening to them and asking them questions. Everyone who heard Him was amazed at His understanding and His answers. When His parents saw Him, they were astonished. His mother said to Him, "Son, why have you treated us like this? Your father and I have been anxiously searching for you." "Why were you searching for me?" He asked. "Didn't you know I had to be in my Father's house?"

Then He went down to Nazareth with them and was obedient to them. But His mother treasured all these things in her heart, and Jesus grew in wisdom and stature, and in favor with God and man.
Luke 2:41-52 (adapted)

THE STORY BEGINS

Words by
LOUIS F. BENSON (1855-1930)

Tune: **KINGSFOLD**
Traditional English Melody
Arranged by
JOSEPH M. MARTIN (BMI)

of the news that came to them from_ an - gels in_ the

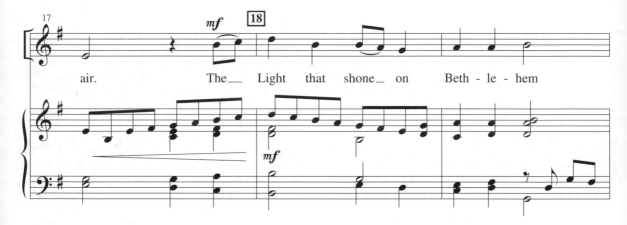

air. The_ Light that shone_ on Beth - le - hem

fills all the world to - day. Of_ Je - sus' birth_ and_

peace on earth,_____ the___ an - gels sing_ al -

Naz - a - reth in each heart may grow.___ Now___

spreads the___ fame___ of___ His dear name on___ all the winds___ that___

blow.

O___

20

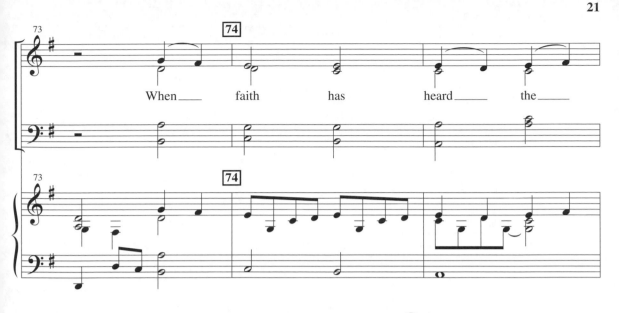

When____ faith has heard____ the____

Mas - ter's____ word,_____

Slower (♩ = ca. 104)

mp unis. (opt. solo)

falls_____ peace up - on____ the

LESSON 3 (Jesus' Ministry Begins)

Filled with the Spirit's power, Jesus returned to Galilee, and a report about Him went throughout all the surrounding country. He taught in their synagogues and was glorified by all. He came to Nazareth, where He had grown up, and as was His custom, He went to the synagogue on the Sabbath day. The scroll of the prophet Isaiah was given to Him to read. He unrolled the scroll and found the place where it was written:

"The Spirit of the Lord is upon me, because He has anointed me to proclaim good news to the poor. He has sent me to proclaim liberty to the captives and recovering of sight to the blind, and to set at liberty those who are oppressed, to proclaim the year of the Lord's favor."

After reading, He rolled up the scroll and gave it back to the attendant and sat down. The eyes of all in the synagogue were fixed on Him as He said to them, "Today this Scripture has been fulfilled in your hearing."
Luke 4:14-24 (adapted)

A DAY OF REJOICING AND PRAISE

Words and music by
JOSEPH M. MARTIN (BMI))

Je - sus is reach - ing the world with His_ love.

Come feel the touch that

Come hear the words of com - fort and prom - ise.

heals the soul. Come to the place where Je - sus is wait - ing.

Come know His grace and be made whole. O____

Je - sus is preach-ing. Je - sus is teach-ing. Je - sus is reach-ing the

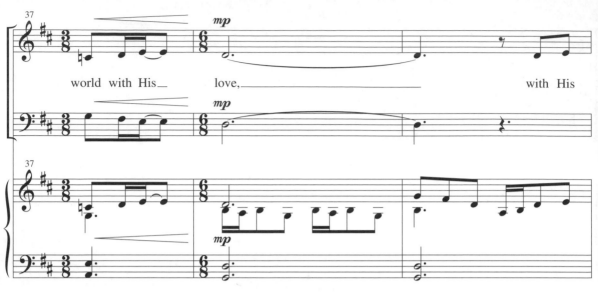

world with His_ love,_____ with His

love._____ The

deaf will hear. The blind will see. The si - lent will speak and the

lame shall leap. The des-ert will blos-som and lift its voice. The

moun-tains and val-leys will all re-joice with a ju-bi-lant noise, a

ju - bi - lant noise. Let the chil-dren sing. Let ho-san-nas ring.

world with His__ love!   Je - sus is preach-ing.

Je - sus is teach-ing.   Je - sus is reach-ing the world_____

with   His   love!

driving with vigor to the end

LESSON 4 (Jesus Enters Jerusalem)

When Jesus drew near to Jerusalem, He sent two of His disciples ahead telling them, "Go into the village and there you will find a colt tethered on which no one has ever sat. Untie it and bring it here. If anyone should say to you, 'Why are you doing this?' reply, 'The Master has need of it and will send it back here at once.'"

So they went off and found a colt tethered at a gate outside on the street, and they untied it. Some of the bystanders said to them, "What are you doing, untying the colt?" They answered just as Jesus had told them to, and were granted permission.

They brought the colt to Jesus and He sat on it. Many people spread their cloaks on the road. Others spread leafy branches that they had cut from the fields. Those preceding Him and those following kept crying out: "Hosanna! Blessed is He who comes in the name of the Lord! Blessed is the kingdom of our father David that is to come! Hosanna in the highest!"
(Mark 11:1-10) adapted

HOSANNA, LOUD HOSANNA

(Congregational Anthem) *

Words by
JENNETTE THRELFALL (1821-1880)

Tune: **ELLACOMBE**
Gesangbuch, Wittenberg, 1784
Arranged by
JOSEPH M. MARTIN (BMI)

* Part for congregation is on page 86.

sim - plest___ and the best. From
on___ His___ bid - ding wait.

mf

cresc. poco a poco

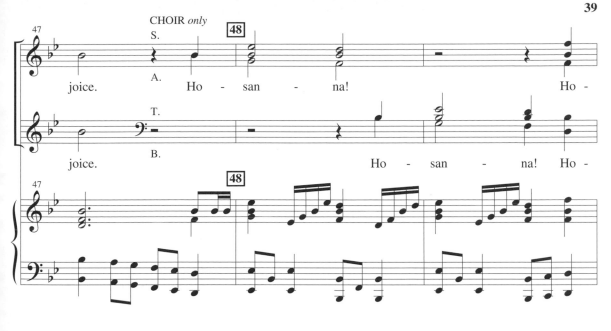

LESSON 5 (The Last Supper)

On the first day of the Festival of Unleavened Bread, the disciples came to Jesus and asked, "Where do you want us to make preparations for You to eat the Passover?"

He replied, "Go into the city to a certain man and tell him, 'The Teacher says: My appointed time is near. I am going to celebrate the Passover with my disciples at your house.'"

So the disciples did as Jesus had directed them and prepared the Passover…

While they were eating, Jesus took bread, and when He had given thanks, He broke it and gave it to His disciples, saying, "Take and eat; this is my body."

Then He took a cup, and when He had given thanks, He gave it to them, saying, "Drink from it, all of you. This is my blood of the covenant, which is poured out for many for the forgiveness of sins. I tell you, I will not drink of this fruit of the vine until that day when I drink it new with you in my Father's kingdom."

When they had sung a hymn, they went out to the Mount of Olives.
Matthew 26:17-30

BANQUET OF MERCY

Words by
REGINALD HEBER (1783-1826)
and **CHARLES H. GABRIEL** (1856-1932)

Music by
JOSEPH M. MARTIN (BMI)
Incorporating tune:
MY SAVIOR'S LOVE
by **CHARLES H. GABRIEL** (1856-1932)

Bread of the world, in mer-cy bro-ken, Wine of the soul, in mer-cy shed,_____

look on the tears by sin - ners shed;

and by Your feast to us the to - ken

that by Your grace our souls are fed.

poco rit.

TESTIMONY OF LIFE - SATB

44

* Tune: MY SAVIOR'S LOVE, Charles H. Gabriel, 1856-1932
Words: Charles H. Gabriel, 1856-1932

TESTIMONY OF LIFE - SATB

46

ev - er be.___ How___ mar-vel-ous! How___ won-der-ful!

is my___ Sav - ior's love for me!_____

(end solo)

and in whose death our sins are dead,

and in whose death our sins are dead.

rit.

LESSON 6 (Gethsemane)

Then Jesus went with His disciples to a place called Gethsemane, and He said to them, "Sit here while I go over there and pray."

Then He said to them, "My soul is overwhelmed with sorrow to the point of death. Stay here and keep watch with me."

Going a little farther, He fell on His face to the ground and prayed, "My Father, if it is possible, may this cup be taken from me. Yet not as I will, but as You will."

Then He returned to His disciples and found them sleeping. "Couldn't you keep watch with me for one hour?" He asked Peter. "Watch and pray so that you will not fall into temptation. The spirit is willing, but the flesh is weak." He went away a second time and prayed, "My Father, if it is not possible for this cup to be taken away unless I drink it, may Your will be done." When He came back, He again found them sleeping, because their eyes were heavy. So He left them and went away once more and prayed the third time, saying the same thing. Then He returned to the disciples and said to them, "Are you still sleeping and resting? Look, the hour has come, and the Son of Man is delivered into the hands of sinners."
Matthew 26:36-45

INTO THE GARDEN

Words by
JOSEPH M. MARTIN (BMI)

Tune: **LANIER**
by PETER LUTKIN (1858-1931)
Arranged by
JOSEPH M. MARTIN (BMI)

54

des - tin - y when in - to the gar - den He went.

Out of the gar - den the Sav - ior went, to climb Gol - go - tha's

LESSON 7 (Jesus is Crucified)

The soldiers led Jesus away to the courtyard of the palace. They clothed Him in a purple cloak, and twisted together a crown of thorns and put it on His head. Then they began to mock Him saying, "Hail, King of the Jews!" They struck His head with a reed and spat upon Him. Finally, they stripped Him of the purple cloak and put His own clothes on Him, and led Him out to be crucified.

They brought Him to the place called Golgotha, meaning "the place of a skull." There, they crucified Him and cast lots among themselves for His clothing. The inscription on His cross read, "The King of the Jews." On either side of Him, they crucified two robbers, one on His right and one on His left. Those who passed by mocked Him, crying, "He saved others but He cannot save Himself."

At noon of that day, it became dark over the entire land and remained that way for three hours. Finally, at three o'clock, Jesus gave a loud cry and breathed His last breath. When a certain centurion saw this, he exclaimed, "Truly this was God's Son."

Mark 15:16-39

WHEN I SURVEY THE WONDROUS CROSS

(Congregational Anthem) *

Words by
ISAAC WATTS (1674-1748)

Tune: **HAMBURG**
by LOWELL MASON (1792-1872)
Arranged by
JOSEPH M. MARTIN (BMI)

* Part for congregation is on page 87.

CHOIR *only*

28 **With great freedom** (♩ = ca. 78)

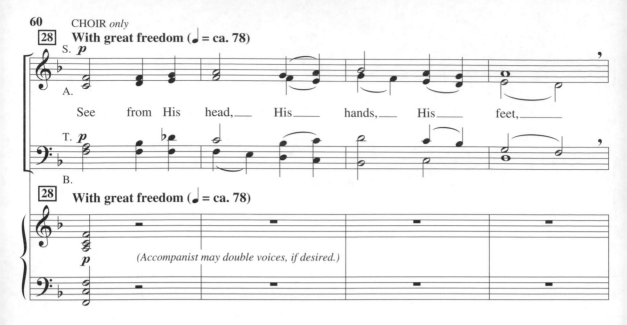

See from His head,___ His___ hands,___ His___ feet,___

28 **With great freedom** (♩ = ca. 78)

(Accompanist may double voices, if desired.)

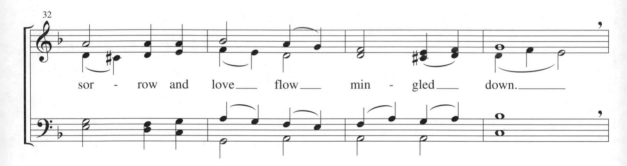

sor - row and love___ flow___ min - gled___ down.___

Did e'er such love___ and___ sor - row___ meet,___

or ___ thorns com - pose___ so rich___ a___ crown?___

rit.

44 **With increasing intensity and passion** (♩ = ca. 88)

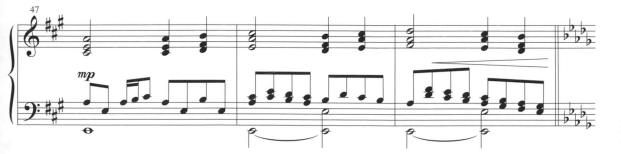

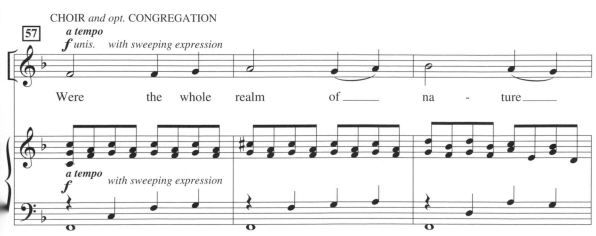

CHOIR *and opt.* CONGREGATION

Were the whole realm of ___ na - ture ___

mine, that were a pres - ent____

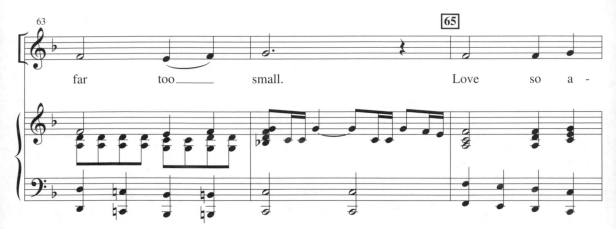

far too____ small. Love so a -

maz - ing,___ so di - vine,

de - mands my soul, my life, my___ all.

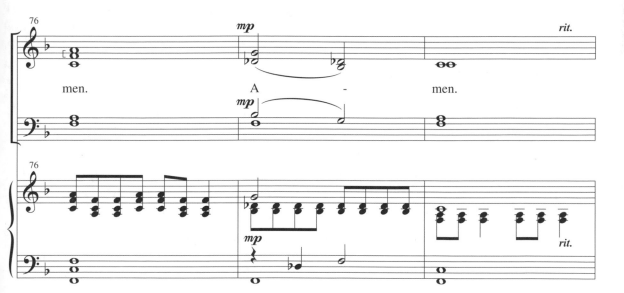

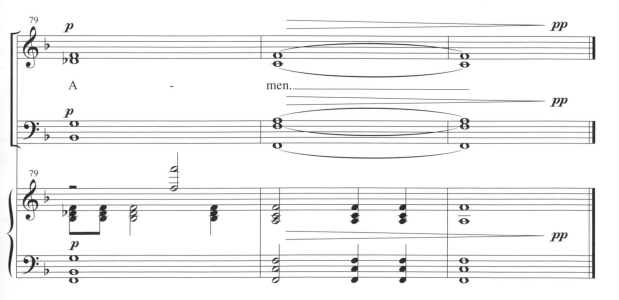

LESSON 8 (Jesus is Risen)

Now after the Sabbath, toward the dawn of the first day of the week, Mary Magdalene and the other Mary went to see Jesus' tomb. Behold, there was a great earthquake, and an angel of the Lord descended from heaven and rolled back the stone. His appearance was like lightning, and His clothing white as snow. The angel said to the women, "Do not be afraid, for I know that you seek Jesus who was crucified. He is not here, for He has risen, as He said. Come, see the place where He lay."
Matthew 28:1-3, 5-6

A DAY BRIGHT WITH JOY

Words: Latin Hymn
Translation by
JOHN MASON NEALE (1818-1866)
Last verse by
JOSEPH M. MARTIN (BMI)

Tune:
PUER NOBIS
Trier Manuscript, 15th Century
Original music amd arrangement by
JOSEPH M. MARTIN (BMI)

66

out_____ with fair - er light, when, to their

long - ing eyes re - stored, the glad A -

pos - tles saw their Lord._____

35

TENOR

BASS

His ris - en flesh with

TESTIMONY OF LIFE - SATB

ra - diance glowed. His wound - ed hands_____ and

feet He showed. Those scars their sol - emn

wit - ness gave that Christ was ris - en

from the grave._____

LESSON 9 (Jesus Appears to the Chosen and Ascends to Heaven)

After His resurrection Jesus appeared to His disciples and opened their minds so they could understand the Scriptures. He told them, "This is what is written: The Messiah will suffer and rise from the dead on the third day. Repentance for the forgiveness of sins will be preached in His name to all nations, beginning at Jerusalem. He then led them out to the vicinity of Bethany; He lifted up His hands and blessed them. While He was blessing them, He was taken up into heaven. They worshipped Him and went on their way with great joy."
Luke 24:45-47,50-52 (adapted)

CLOSING PRAYER *(can be read before or after the last song)*

Risen Christ, Living Lord, renew us by Your resurrection power. May the miracles of Your life and ministry live and work through Your people. May Your church be a reflection of Your light, and may that Light shine in the darkness as a reminder of Your love and mercy. May Your wondrous story be proclaimed in word and deed to all peoples. May the music of Your grace echo through time as a testimony to Your everlasting life! AMEN!

I KNOW THAT MY REDEEMER LIVES

(Congregational Anthem) *

Words by
SAMUEL MEDLEY (1738-1799)

Tune: **DUKE STREET**
by JOHN HATTON (1710-1793)
Arranged by
JOSEPH M. MARTIN (BMI)

* Part for congregation is on page 88.

CHOIR *and opt.* CONGREGATION

I know that my Re - deem - er___ lives!
He lives, tri - um - phant___ from___ the___ grave.
He lives, my kind, wise___ heav'n - ly___ friend.

What com - fort this as - sur - ance gives!
He lives, e - ter - nal - ly___ to___ save.
He lives and loves me___ to___ the___ end.

He lives. He lives___ who___ once___ was___ dead.
He lives ex - alt - ed,___ throned___ a - bove.
He lives, and while___ He___ lives,___ I'll___ sing.

TESTIMONY OF LIFE - SATB

He lives, my ev - er - liv - ing___ Head!
He lives to rule___ His church in___ love.
He lives, my Proph - et, Priest and___ King!

Maestoso (♩ = ca. 100)

SOPRANO DESCANT

Let ev - 'ry crea - ture___ rise and___

CHOIR *and opt.* CONGREGATION
f unis.

Let ev - 'ry crea - ture___ rise and___

Maestoso (♩ = ca. 100)

82

I WILL SING THE WONDROUS STORY

Words by
FRANCIS H. ROWLEY (1854-1952)

Tune: **HYFRYDOL**
by ROWLAND H. PRICHARD (1811-1887)
Arranged by
JOSEPH M. MARTIN (BMI)

I was lost,_____ but Je - sus found _____ me;
Days of dark - ness still_____ come o'er _____ me.
Yes, I'll sing_____ the won - drous sto - ry

found the sheep_____ that went _____ a - stray,_____
Sor - row's paths_____ I of - ten tread;_____
of the Christ_____ who died _____ for me. _____

threw _____ His lov - ing arms_____ a - round_____ me,
but _____ the Sav - ior still_____ is with _____ me.
Sing _____ it with _____ the saints _____ in glo - ry,

drew _____ me back _____ in - to His way.
By _____ His hand _____ I'm safe - ly led.
gath - ered by _____ the crys - tal sea.

TESTIMONY OF LIFE - SATB

HOSANNA, LOUD HOSANNA

Words by
JENNETTE THRELFALL (1821-1880)

Tune: **ELLACOMBE**
Gesangbuch, Wittenberg, 1784
Arranged by
JOSEPH M. MARTIN (BMI)

TESTIMONY OF LIFE - SATB

WHEN I SURVEY THE WONDROUS CROSS

Words by
ISAAC WATTS (1674-1748)

Tune: **HAMBURG**
by LOWELL MASON (1792-1872)
Arranged by
JOSEPH M. MARTIN (BMI)

CONGREGATION *unison*

cong. 1. When I sur - vey the won - drous cross,
cong. 2. For - bid it, Lord, that I should boast,
choir 3. See from His head, His hands, His feet,
cong. 4. Were the whole realm of na - ture mine,

on which the Prince of glo - ry died,
save in the death of Christ, my God.
sor - row and love flow min - gled down.
that were a pres - ent far too small.

my rich - est gain I count but loss,
All the vain things that charm me most,
Did e'er such love and sor - row meet,
Love so a - maz - ing, so di - vine,

and pour con - tempt on all my pride.
I sac - ri - fice them to His blood.
or thorns com - pose so rich a crown.
de - mands my soul, my life, my all.

I KNOW THAT MY REDEEMER LIVES

Words by
SAMUEL MEDLEY (1738-1799)

Tune: **DUKE STREET**
by JOHN HATTON (1710-1793)
Arranged by
JOSEPH M. MARTIN (BMI)

CONGREGATION

parts 1. I know that my Re - deem - er ___ lives!
parts 2. He lives, tri - um - phant ___ from ___ the ___ grave.
parts 3. He lives, my kind, wise ___ heav'n - ly ___ friend.
unis. 4. Let ev - 'ry crea - ture ___ rise ___ and ___ bring,

What com - fort this as - sur - ance gives!
He lives, e - ter - nal - ly to ___ save.
He lives and loves me to ___ the ___ end.
bless - ing and hon - or ___ to ___ our King.

He lives. He lives ___ who ___ once ___ was ___ dead.
He lives ex - alt - ed, ___ throned ___ a - bove.
He lives, and while ___ He ___ lives, ___ I'll ___ sing.
An - gels de - scend ___ with ___ songs ___ a - gain;

He lives, my ev - er - liv - ing ___ Head!
He lives to rule His church in ___ love.
He lives, my Proph - et, Priest and ___ King!
and earth re - peats ___ the loud a - men!

TESTIMONY OF LIFE - SATB